do not cut out
white areas between
arms and body

H

Tom Tierney

Henry VIII

Plate 1

Catherine of Aragon was born in 1485, the daughter of Ferdinand and Isabella of Spain. To cement an alliance between England and Spain, she was married at age 15 to Arthur, age 14, eldest son of King Henry VII . When Arthur died in 1502, after a year of marriage, she was betrothed to young Henry. They were wed when he ascended the throne, in 1509.

As Henry VIII's first wife, Catherine served as England's regent for nearly 15 years while Henry waged war in France. Although Catherine bore him six children, five of whom died in infancy, she did not provide him with a male heir, which displeased Henry. They were both Catholic, so divorce was impossible. Henry sought an annulment from the Pope, Catherine's cousin, which was denied. This triggered Henry's split from the Catholic Church, and his subsequent establishment of the Church of England. Henry, as head of this new church, dissolved the marriage himself.

Henry forced Catherine to live in virtual penury during her last years. When she died in 1536, it was rumored that her death had been hastened by a sip of a "certain Welsh beer."

Catherine of Aragon

Plate 2

Plate 3

Henry VIII

Plate 4

Anne Boleyn was the second wife of Henry VIII and the mother of the future Queen Elizabeth I. Anne was born around 1507; her father was Sir Thomas Boleyn. Spending her childhood in France, at age fifteen, she returned to live in Henry's court. Although not known as a great beauty, she had many admirers. Henry and Anne's liaison began six years prior to the end of his marriage to Catherine of Aragon. He had married Anne five months before the annulment in 1533; four months later Anne gave birth to Princess Elizabeth. In 1536 she bore him a stillborn son. Blaming her for not producing a viable male heir, Henry lost interest in her and had liaisons with several other women. Anne's fits of jealousy, and what the court interpreted as arrogant behavior, made her unpopular. Five months after the stillbirth, Henry had her committed to the Tower of London on the charge of adultery. She was found guilty and beheaded on May 19, 1536. Approximately ten days later, Henry married Jane Seymour.

Anne Boleyn

Plate 5

Plate 6

Jane Seymour was Henry VIII's third wife and the mother of his heir, King Edward VI. She was born in approximately 1509. Jane Seymour's father was Sir John Seymour of Wolf Hall, Savernake, Wiltshire. She was sent to court to serve as a lady-in-waiting, first to Catherine of Aragon and then to Anne Boleyn. Around 1535 Henry proposed she become his mistress. Her insistence on marriage may have precipitated the downfall of Anne Boleyn.

On May 30, 1536 they were married in a private ceremony. At her urging, Henry's daughter by Catherine of Aragon, Mary, (though still a Catholic) was restored to the King's favor.

After 17 months of marriage, she bore Henry his long desired male heir. To Henry's great sorrow, Jane Seymour died 12 days later, on October 24, 1537, of post childbirth complications. Her family enjoyed the king's favor until the end of his days. Edward was 10 years old when his father died. He ruled from 1547–53.

Jane Seymour

Plate 7

Plate 8

Henry VIII

Tom Tierney

H

Plate 9

Anne of Cleves, Henry VIII's fourth wife, was born September 22, 1515 in Germany. Having attained his male heir, Henry now wanted a wife who would be a political asset to help counter a threat from France and the Holy Roman Empire. The marriage was arranged by Anne's brother William, Duke of Cleves, the leader of the Lutheran Protestants. At age twenty-five, Anne arrived in London to meet her fiancé for the first time. Five days later, three years after the death of Jane Seymour, they were wed.

His new bride was neither as pretty nor as sophisticated as Henry had been led to believe. She spoke little English. When the threat from Henry's Catholic enemies failed to materialize, the marriage seemed a mistake. Anne acquiesced and the marriage was annulled. She was rewarded with a large income, her own castle, and occasional visits to the court where she was given the status of Henry's sister. She died in London on July 16, 1557.

Anne of Cleves

Plate 10

do not cut out
white areas between
arms and body

AC

AC

Plate 11

Henry VIII's fifth wife was **Catherine Howard**. Born about 1525, not only is her true birth date unknown, there is no properly authenticated portrait of her. The likeness here is based on a portrait that is often cited as her picture.

Catherine was one of 10 children; her father was Lord Edmund Howard. Henry first noticed her as a young girl as he was ending his marriage to Anne of Cleves. Nineteen days after the annulment, he married Catherine Howard. For the next year he seemed much enamored with his new bride, but in November of 1541 he learned that Catherine had participated in several affairs prior to their marriage. Henry was furious. On February 11, 1542 Parliament passed a bill of attainder declaring it illegal for an unchaste woman to marry the king. Two days later, Catherine was beheaded in the Tower of London.

Catherine Howard

Plate 12

do not cut out
white area between
arm and body

CH

CH

Plate 13

Catherine Parr was Henry VIII's sixth wife. Born in 1512, her father was Sir Thomas Parr, an official in the royal household. Catherine had been widowed twice before her marriage to Henry in July of 1543. Her kindness and tact enabled her to nurse the ailing king and to exert a beneficial influence on him. She developed close friendships with Henry's three surviving children and devoted herself to their education. Catherine attempted to mitigate the persecution of Catholics in England, a dangerous political path. She is known to have narrowly escaped being accused of heresy by flattering the king. After Henry's death she married a former suitor, but died in 1548 at age 36, shortly after giving birth to a daughter.

TOM TIERNEY

Catherine Parr

Plate 14

do not cut out
white areas between
arms and body

CP

CP

Plate 15

This costume is for Henry VIII on Plate 9.

Plate 16